Songs
and
Letters

Rosanna Lowther-Berman

ISBN 978-1-965679-07-4 (Paperback)
ISBN 978-1-965679-08-1 (Ebook)

Inquiries and Book Orders should be addressed to:

Leavitt Peak Press
17901 Pioneer Blvd Ste L #298, Artesia, California 90701
Phone #: 2092191548

Dedicated to Stanford D. Berman

His life is a quiet mitzvah.
Caring when other don't care;
Angry at any injustice
Even if he's treated fair.

His life is a quiet mitzvah.
Loving the poor and distressed;
Giving without reservation
Of all that is his, of his best.

His life is a quiet mitzvah.
And my greatest blessing in life
Is the duty and joy…is the honor…
Is the privilege of being his wife.

CONTENTS

Epistle to the Americans

CHAPTER I

Dear friends,

The times we live in are difficult, and we are unsure of many things. These words are sent to you so that you might remember the things you are sure of.

We are sure of the love of God.

We may know God in different ways, even as my child knows me differently than you. Yet both you and my child know the same being, even though neither of you knows me completely.

So do not disdain or condemn another because of the way he or she knows God.

This is as if my child should condemn you because I am not your parent. None of us knows God completely; we are none of us big enough for that.

And we know that God teaches us to love each other and respect one another, so respect the different ways that others love God.

God is love.

If the God you know teaches hate, not love, then it is not God you know.

Constantly try to get to know God better, to reach out toward heaven, even as God reaches out to you.

God will always help you grow and reach.

The person you should most pity and pray for is the person who does not try to grow, reach, and know. This person cannot know God.

Perhaps he or she believes they have all the answers about God.

But love is a process, never-ending. We can never know all about the infinite God.

Perhaps he or she does not believe in God. This person cannot know God.

You cannot understand something you do not believe in; you can only fantasize about it.

Therefore, strive to know God better every day. Keep in touch and continue to reach out.

It is easy to accept others' opinions about God. Many people do this.

They do not strive to know God themselves. Instead, they let others tell them what they should know about God.

These people are lost and confused when someone points out discrepancies in their secondhand knowledge. They cannot refer to "the God I know."

You must have a strong personal relationship with God. You must personally know.

Then when others try to confuse you with their own second-hand knowledge, saying, "God hates Jews or Muslims or African Americans," you can say, "Not the God I know!"

I need to talk to you about asking.

Do not be afraid to ask God for anything. I have never known God to not listen to such prayers.

But always remember to ask God to do what is best for you, not what you, with imperfect wisdom, may want.

Then you can leave your request with God, and know that whatever the answer is, it is best for you. It may not be what you want, but it is best.

Having done this, be very careful to accept what God sends you.

Do not ask, but then if the response is not what you wanted, try to create or manipulate the world to get what you want.

When we do this, we insult God.

The outcome is never good.

I tell you this because I know this, having erred this way when I did not know God so well.

CHAPTER 2

The nature of God is love.

Please remember that anytime any person claims that God acts or wants you to act without love, that person does not speak for God.

God, this wonderful incomprehensible God that we serve and seek, is love.

Love does not kill; it dies first.

Love does not hate; it pities and helps.

Love does not force change, for it knows that change always comes from within.

Change that is not a free action is coercion. God never coerces. God waits.

First. We must seek God first, or we do not find God at all.

No good comes from actions done without love.

Be sure that all your actions are done with love.

There is no other acceptable reason—not self-preservation, not revenge, not punishment, not education.

Seek to know the God of love. Seek to act always in love.

And when you fail, as we all do, know that the God of love waits for you to try again.

Perhaps you will get it right the next time. Certainly, the trying will bring you closer to that Perfect Love, which is God.

Dear people, people beloved of God (as all people are), do not forget that to know God is to grow.

If the God you know is the same God you knew a year ago, or ten years ago—if the God you know is the same God your ancestors knew—then you are not growing.

Therefore, do not be afraid of growing and changing the way you know God.

Do not be afraid when others around you change the way they know God.

Change is growth if it brings you closer to the God that is love.

Rather, worry and speak to God often on behalf of those who do not grow or who regress in their knowing. These poor souls have slipped backward in knowledge.

There are some who, knowing a God of love, choose instead to call their God by many names, to give God attributes of nature or humans.

It should be the opposite. We should see in nature and humanity the attributes of God.

Make no mistake. There is one God, one being who permeates and controls the universe.

There are those who have never known God by one name as one being.

If that is how they have always known God, that relationship is between them and God.

You and I have nothing to do with it.

But there are also those who have known God by one name as one being.

When they choose to relate to God as an aspect of nature, they negate the universality and the power of the one God.

It is as if your friend suddenly treats you as if you were a stranger or did not exist at all!

Think how this must sadden God.

Think how these people have denied themselves the joy of a more complete knowledge of God and have chosen a poorer understanding.

You must strive to always grow in the knowledge of God. You must expect that knowledge to change and grow, not stagnate or reverse.

Talk to God, and God will talk to you.

Do not be afraid of God's voice; rather, be afraid if you never hear it.

The more you listen, and the more you talk, the easier it will be for you to know God's voice and to distinguish it from others who tell you to act and think a certain way.

The more you listen, and the more you talk, the easier it will be for you to know God's voice and to distinguish it from your own voice, telling you what you want to hear.

Talk to God, and God will talk to you.

Do not think of talking to God as prayer.

Too often, we see prayer as a petition.

Your knowledge of God comes from direct communication, both you and God in blessed talk!

Of course, tell God your problems, your concerns, your joys, and your hopes.

Rest assured that as you love God, so God loves you.

Those things that happen that we perceive as bad are really for our good. I believe this.

As we grow, we begin to understand this more, even as we trust God more with ourselves and our corporate and individual destinies.

Never underestimate the power of God.

Never underestimate the power of God within you.

It is only by believing in what we cannot see that we see what we believe.

Remember to trust God to be on your side, any time that what you do does not hurt and does good.

But be very wary of any act, however noble or selfless, that hurts another.

We are not wise enough or strong enough to judge when it is right to inflict hurt on another. This is the sole prerogative of God.

Dear friends, we all have times when our decisions might hurt another. To decide is to hurt; to not decide is to hurt.

When these times come, when it is your role to judge, do not be afraid of that.

God has placed you in that situation so that you might act as God would act.

Pray that you are living so close to God and that your decisions and actions will mimic those of your God.

Live in this peace.

But above all, love.

CHAPTER 3

Do not be afraid of yourself. If you are not your dearest friend, then work hard to make yourself so.

The evil outside of you is nothing compared to the evil that lies within. Like cancer, it can mimic your own good self so that even you cannot recognize it.

It is easy to hate, feel disgusted, be arrogant, or be condescending. None of these come from the good God has placed in you.

God has given you your body and your soul. You must tend and nurture them both.

When you abuse your body by feeding it that which is not good for it, you insult God's gift.

When you abuse your body by not keeping it clean and healthy, you insult God's gift.

When you abuse your soul by feeding it that which is not good for it, you insult God's gift.

When you abuse your soul by not keeping it clean and healthy, you insult God's gift.

How do we so abuse ourselves? There are many ways, and each one of us has a weakness, a thing that is our temptation for abuse.

For some, it is food, for some drink, for some pornography, for some mindless entertainment, for some exercise, for some gambling, for some religious fervor. The list is as varied, as there are bodies and souls.

Excess in anything corrupts the body and the soul. Even love, when it is excessive, corrupts the soul.

Strive to keep God's gifts to you free from corruption. No one does this perfectly. All must try.

Be at peace within yourself. If you cannot love the person you are now, you cannot change that person.

Do not believe those who tell you that you cannot change. The ability to change is God's greatest gift to people.

In a world where change is the only constant, it is easy to condemn it, to wish for a world without change.

Just as your life is a journey, so all must change. This is good. It is not to be feared.

Fear rather ideas and people who do not change.

CHAPTER 4

I cannot emphasize enough how necessary it is for you to remain in constant communication with God.

This is the only way to grow and learn. No amount of ritual attendance, no amount of profession of faith, and no amount of good deeds will substitute.

The foundation of faith is communication with God.

Ask of God. Believe the answers. Receive of God. Believe in God's love.

There are those who will tell you to pray. Prayer is like a letter to God. It has a beginning, middle, and end. It is a ritual.

No. Communicate with God. Listen for answers. Ask questions. Let your life be one constant conversation with your Deity. Let God teach you.

I am a teacher. I am a poet. But I am first a conversant with God. This is my most essential function. This is my essence. This is how I grow and learn and live eternally.

For there is no death in this conversation. There is only life and joy and beauty.

Therefore, strive to know your God, secretly and publicly. Listen. Learn. Live.

Beware of anger and hate. Beware of apathy. Beware of any emotion that leaves you uncaring about others. Even love itself should be shunned if it limits our ability to love.

Whatever you do, do it with love.

A word of caution here. Love does not change. When you love something or someone you do not want to change it or them. You do not make demands.

Beware of any person, organization, or teaching that tells you it wants to change you because it loves you. It does not love you; it wants you to do or behave the way it wants.

No matter how noble sounding its aims, no matter how beautifully intense its message, if you must change to continue in its love, well that is not love!

Unfortunately, some religious groups do this. They say, "We love you, but to receive our love, to be helped by us, you must do what we say."

Dear friends, this is not love.

It is coercion. There is no love there. There is control. There is a self-righteous "I can live your life better than you can" philosophy.

There is no love.

Think about this. When you love someone, what do you want to do? You want to change yourself to please them. You want to change the world to please them. The last thing you want is to change them.

This is the secret of love. It is its greatest strength, as well as its greatest weakness.

When you love someone, you are the one who changes.

The only real change happens because of love.

Love must be there first; then there can be change. Coerced change, however positive it appears, always rots away from the inside out, like a plant given too much water. If its essence of self has not changed from the inside; then no amount of behavior changing will keep it alive.

Each individual "you" must love God first, and then you can reach out to both God and the world. Then you can forgive and love each other.

We are witnessing a great sham in our beloved country and world today. Some people hate and justify it with religion, with their love of God!

There are people, leaders, who go to war because they are compassionate. What is this? I will kill you and your children so I can help you.

There is no love there. There is no God there.

There are people, leaders, who go to war because they hate their enemy. At least this is honest.

But there is no love there. There is no God there.

CHAPTER 5

There is a great temptation for any religion when it is culturally or politically powerful to equate itself with good government.

This is always wrong. It can grow to be evil. It is really very easy for people to kill, maim, or hurt in the name of love.

God have mercy on us all.

Dear friends, government and religion are like oil and vinegar. They do not mix.

There is a very real reason for this.

We know that love is God, and the seeking and knowing of God result in love for others. It results in mercy, peace, and kindness. This is real religion, whatever the name of its God.

But the essence of government is law. It is safety, the preservation of power. In its highest form, it is justice. Justice is the real government, whatever the name of its social system.

Justice and love will always disagree.

You have only to look at history to see how absurd our arguments become when we try to mix these two.

Can you imagine a just religion? It would not exist long because its followers would have a duty to commit suicide.

People who try to mix religion and government really are saying that they want religion, love, and mercy for their group, government, and justice and no love or mercy for everyone else.

I am sorry for I have written much too long a letter.

Please forgive me, but I was burdened with these words.

There are those who will criticize these words, and that is all right.

Just remember, we are more alike than different.

Just remember, love.

Try to have more love in your life.

Communicate with God.

And you will not need to seek peace, for you will live it.

Blessings upon you!

Epistle to the Children

------- ◆◆◆◆◆ -------

We who are your elders and know so little salute you, the children, who know so much!

You are clean and free and unbiased. You judge the world by who is good to you and who is not.

You will equate evil with him who is not and good with him who is. May it always be so.

Later, when you are older, your parents will want to change that.

They will say that evil is what they say it is and good is sometimes hurtful.

Do not believe them. Trust the God within you.

The sooner you learn that your parents are the last people to tell you the truth, the wiser you will be.

This is not because they are bad. It is not because they do not love you.

It is just the opposite. They lie to you because they love you.

They want, far more than they want your happiness, for you to be like them.

But make no mistake; if you are like them, then the world cannot become better than it is. After all, they are the way the world is.

So strive to learn from your parents. Master the art of silent disagreement. Learn from your friends. Master the art of caring. Learn from the God within you. Master the art of divine intimacy.

And in all things, learn and grow. You cannot learn and not grow.

This is why so many people, your parents foremost, will try to limit the things you learn.

They want to prune you like a tree so that you will grow in only a certain way.

Dear little children, be a wilderness oak! Grow wild and tall and free!

Be constrained only by the nature God has given you, your intellect, your physical being.

Learn, always learn!

Do not be surprised when you become someone different from your parents. Be glad!

There are those who will try to convince you that they are the smartest because they yell the loudest.

Remember this:

The deaf are far more blessed than anyone with hearing.

Their ears are tuned exclusively to hear the voice of God.

The credible are quiet. There are too many preachers

Who hide a fake religion behind a loud facade.

There are those who will try to convince you that they are the smartest because they are the oldest.

Remember this:

Age is no guarantee of anything but aging.

Wisdom counts some of her children among the very young.

There are those who will try to convince you that they are the smartest because they have the most money.

Remember this:

Things don't count, people do.

No one who can be bought is worth buying.

There are those who will try to convince you that they are the smartest because they have gone to school the longest.

Remember this:
The things you learn the very best
Are things you teach yourself.
The only real function of a school
Is to teach you to teach yourself.

Beware! Learning is lonely. Thinking is hard. It is easier to just memorize and repeat. No one wants you to question him or her or what he or she believes. They do not mind if you repeat what they say. But if you do that, you are not learning; you are just repeating.

Do not spend your life repeating someone else's life. Make your life better than theirs! Think your own thoughts! Be you! Listen to the God within you!

Listen to the God within you, even when you are punished for it.

It is only by listening and learning this way that you grow.

Do not be afraid. God is with you. God is in you. Be at peace.

Seek peace in all you do. Fighting and quarreling are not God's way. Thinking and learning are God's way.

Hubris

———— ✦ ✦ ✦ ✦ ✦ ————

There is nothing sadder than a man who believes he hears God but only hears his own echo.

This man cannot be reasoned with, for he truly believes that his own wishes are the wishes of God.

Only God can deal with such a man. Only God is willing to deal with such a man. Such a man must be pitied, for the justice of God is to be feared. It is most merciful, but it is also divinely just.

How then can anyone say he or she hears the voice of God?

How can one know the difference between the voice of God and the echo of internal wishes?

Dear friend, remember what we know about God.

We know that God is.

We know that God is within each of us.

We know that God is love, only love, nothing but love.

We know, therefore, that any "voice," any idea, that does not reflect love is not of God.

It may be a noble thought. It may be a just thought. But if that thought lacks love, then it is not of God.

This is why it is so sad when people say that god told them to kill or that god told them to go to war. There is no love in killing. There may be mercy, but no love. There may be a warped sense of justice, but no love. There is no love in killing. There is no love in war.

It is really so easy, dear friend, to know the voice of God.

Ah, but it is so difficult, too, to realize that. Much as we want God to say certain things, God does not speak except in love.

Then beware most of yourself. The thing that drives people from God is themselves individually. It is not other religions, for all religions can lead to God. It is not hatred, for hatred will eventually self-destruct. It is not fear, for fear is merely a lack of faith.

No, we are without God when we are most intensely occupied with ourselves.

Your wants, your needs, your self—these things are the things that keep you from God, that keep you from hearing the voice of God.

And make no mistake; these things can mask themselves as the "voice" of god.

And make no mistake; you will want them to do so!

This is why the real test of the voice and wants of God is, and always was, LOVE.

It is so sad to see people mistake their own pride for the voice of God. Frequently, these people are trying to serve God, but they become confused by their own needs and wants.

It is easy to say to yourself: I am good. I try to serve God. Therefore, what I want is what God must want.

If I want a bigger church, if I want the destruction of my enemies, if I want a child, if I want money, if…well, God must want these things for me too. These things must be the will of God.

Unfortunately, these people frequently find a religious teacher or priest who will confirm their feelings.

These priests or preachers tell their followers, "You must only follow what I say: Don't drink alcohol. Don't gamble. And always wear green socks on Tuesday" (or some other such dictum).

They say, "Follow me, and everything will be all right. Do what I say, and you will go to heaven!"

Always, always sooner or later, these preachers are wrong. The poor follower does what he or she is told, and still everything is not all right.

Why? Firstly, because heaven, like God, is within you.

Heaven is living with God.

Hell is the absence of God.

So you see, heaven either is, or it is not. It is not something that is going to be. If it is, it is now.

Secondly, while we live on this earth, bad things will happen to us. People die. There are injuries, accidents, cruelty, and neglect. Some of these things are the result of the actions of people. Some are the result of natural events. But they happen to all of us.

No matter how many rules we follow (don't' drink alcohol; don't gamble; and always wear green socks on Tuesday), bad things will happen.

Some followers become despondent. They leave the preacher, and they may leave their religion for another religion.

But the problem is not their religion; it is that they have depended on the preacher/imam/priest to know the will of God for them.

They have not touched the God within them.

They have not realized that the only real rule for living is this: "love."

They would rather depend on ritual and a shaman. They would rather not grow with God.

We must remember the song:

> There are times when the mercy of God is a sword
> And you bleed as its sets your heart free.
> For the touch of the Master can sometimes bring
>   fire
> As he molds us to what we should be.
> We must never forget that our Lord's only goal
> Is to gather His own to His side.
> And our blistering agony's born of ourselves
> For we don't want what He will provide.
> If we follow, He leads. But He loves us far more.
> When we choose our own way, He explains
> If we only seek shelter with Him in the storm
> We will dwell in perpetual rains.

The growth sometimes is painful.

The growth can create an even greater temptation. We can begin to see ourselves as priests and preachers. Many do this.

They take money from the poor in the name of the church. They let others support them while they make more rules and promises of eternal life.

They mistake their own voice for the voice of God.

May God protect me from myself and from the evil in the world and in me.

Songs

WHY NOW?

Why now? This outburst of creative sound?
The silence was a friend I learned to love,
That minor music, senseless yet profound,
Which I could mask but never rise above.

Why now? This unsolicited response
To muses nameless, or with names profane.
Oh, leave, dark spirit, all my being haunts
Recesses far beyond where pride has lain.

Why now? I am content in discontent.
My sight adjusts to paths I cannot know.
And if I know not roads where I am sent,
At least I trust enough to let life go.

Why now? I know not. Specter that is me
Arise from ashes of the yet to be.

CHILDREN

How nice to have a messy home!
It tells of people living there
And children playing noisily.
The clutter of a filled-up house.

No sadder dwelling than the one
So clean and neat and everywhere
The ghosts of children grown and gone,
The tears for a departed spouse.

*Only when the future has no relevance are we sometimes given
the ability to see the future. Affinity clouds sight.

MEA CULPA

O Deity that knows my name
I rest my weary self in thee.
For all thy blessings I would claim
Thy lovely plans I, careless, main
Oh, pardon me.

Oh, Teacher-Friend by whom I've grown
I leave my wasted mind with thee.
For all the evil I have known
The unused talent I have shown
Oh, pardon me.

Oh, Savior God who holds me dear,
I leave my future safe with thee.
Instill the love that clams all fear
And let me dwell forever near
To love, to thee.

*We, the people, will never be truly civilized until our monuments to peace outnumber our monuments to war (Gettysburg, March 30, 1995).

Judas

I did not know until I left her arms,
The magnitude of comfort that was mine.
Until I knew those who did not know her
I little guessed how much made her divine.

I did not know until I knew a world
Without her blessed presence, just how bare
A life could be. How could I comprehend
A state of being where she did not care?

I did not know. Forgive me, precious God.
I took for granted all she had to give.
I did not know how much I needed her
Or how her living gave me the strength to live.

I did not know. But seeing how a man
Attempts to cope with life without her love
And fails most sadly, now I realize
The awful sin that I am guilty of.

I did not know. For she had long been mine.
Her faith, her hope, she taught, and I betrayed.
I did not know until I knew despair.
I did not know until my choice was made.

WHO KEEPS IT NEAT

Who keeps it neat,
Her little space.
Who keeps it sterile,
Void of mess.
She keeps it to herself. To share
Requires some rules to be sacrificed.

Who keeps it neat,
She keeps it lone
And revels in
Its cleanliness.
She keeps it pretty, elegant,
And underneath it all, the tears.

*If the God you know teaches hate, not love,
    then it is not God you know.
*The evil most difficult to recognize is the evil closest to home.

Good Friday II

Raped,
Violated,
Everything you ever believed in
Impregnated with all the vile filth you so despised.
Welling up,
Growing,
Inside you until that awful grotesqueness
Consumes you.
Almost becomes who you really are.

This is the cross.
This is why
I cannot volunteer my life for another.
I am not mine to die.
I am His,
The Deity who was raped for me.
The violation of the holy.
The rape of God.

As Out of the Pit

O Christ, beyond my desp'rate thoughts
I sense a gloom unstained by light.
I fear tomorrow's sunless day.
I fear far more death's endless night.

The Gordian groping of my soul
From time to time, it seems, must writhe.
Yet I look upward, and you are home
As out of the pit I rise.

Oh, throbbing, cursed memories
Betray my reason to my heart.
Avoiding madness, I embrace
The rational with ardent art.

When intellect and passion merge
The outcome borders paradise.
And I look upward where you are home,
As out of the pit I rise.

SAD EYES

Sad eyes against tomorrow,
I give what I can give.
Your days bring only sorrow.
I strive that you might live.

Can I know if your living
Which seems so sad to me
To you approaches heaven,
Or carnal ecstasy?

*Those who devote their lives to lust
    And leave love lying in the dust
    Are doomed to lose what they would keep
    And at devotion's grave to weep.

CLEAN

A church should cleanse itself before
It tries to cleanse the world.
To try the second first ensures
Success attained at neither.
To try the second first ensures
That evil still prevails.

*No one can fight with God and win.
　God has the power to make your sin
　The tool that leads you to repent.
　Rejection is God's instrument.

*It is impolite to bother the dead if they do not bother you.
(Corollary: Those who bother the dead are bothered.) Romney,
WV 2/97

MOURNING

And spring has no pleasure now,
And time no sweet promises,
For all that died as you died.
Forgive me my blasphemy.
Forgive me, my mother,
For spring has no pleasure now,
And time no sweet promises.

*When we are children, school is our life. All our friends, and the greater part of our day, are wrapped around school. The idea of life that is not somehow tied to "school" is unimaginable. Yet as we grow older, our perception changes. "School" does not. Rather, we finally see that "school" is only one small fragment of our life, and that life comprises so much more than "school."

I think that we will, sometime after death, view life the way a child views school.

THIS WIZENED SHELL

This wizened shell that once held joy,
Until it knew that men could lie,
Until it knew that people die,
Until it knew perpetual pain.
The miracle of love is this:
This wizened shell that once held joy,
That once knew childhood gay and free,
And thought the world a holy place…
This wizened shell that once held joy,
And gradually was drained of joy,
(Which is another word for life)
And suddenly was dry and dead…
This wizened shell that once held joy,
Now breathes again and laughs again,
And loves again. Praise God.

Epitaph (My Own)

Envy me my life.
It was much better than I deserved.
Envy me my death,
United in perfect love.

GOOD FRIDAY

He will not see the sky again
As man, that swirling gray and blue.
He lies flat on his back. His back
Excruciating, throbs, recoils,
The prelude of the pain to come.

Last night, he wept water and blood.
Water and blood, "Thy will, not mine."
The aftermath of sins erased
With blood and pain and desperate love.

The father's will drives deep the nails.
The love of Jesus cries, "Drive on!"

*It is not the evil without that kills; no, child, it's the evil within.

Unpardonable

Complacency's the greatest sin.
At least the doomed evaluate
The status quo, however bleak,
Alternatives can contemplate.

But those who see no need for change
Perceive the present as success,
And they who cannot error see
Die unrepentant, pardonless.

CONCRETE

The concrete yields to abstract where
The streets of reason end in prayer,
And if the Hounds of Heaven pursue
'Tis sure Hell's Huntsman follows too.

*Cynicism in a poet is fatal.

SOLUS REVISITED

The sun does not shine today.
Why?
Fog, gray fog, covers the river.

A man's brain is gray
So they say.

Gray brains, gray brains,
Running around in a circle.
One circle, two circles,
Two hundred years of circles.
See one circle. White brain!
1860.
See one circle. White brain!
1776.

The sun does not shine today.
Why?
Fog, gray fog, covers the river.

SAGA

One million ladies
In nylon stockings,
Their hair piled high,
Their makeup on,
Parade down.

One million men
Run a race.
Run, see, run!
Their ties are on,
Their shirts are right,
They run a race.

Five hundred thousand children
Sit in a corner.
And cry. Their hands
Held out, in supplication,
Their hearts begging for love.

One million ladies
Stop and pet them.

One million men
Throw them money
Because everyone else does.

Five hundred thousand children
"Rise and call them blessed"?
Ha!
Five hundred thousand children
Rebel.

There is a road filled with blood.
There is a river deep and wide.
And the piper plays.

Dialogue from *George*

Good man of ancient lineage, come you here?
Shall you settle in the court of George the Third
And to your endless travels give an end?

Not now, my lord.

As so. But well, it is that you
Did choose this night to come
For I am tired of cares besetting day
And haunting all my rooms in deepest night.
Come speak. I am wise enough to know you did not come
To say that I look well for wealth alone.

My lord, I come, for traveler I am
And as a traveler, having seen the coasts
Of all the distant colonies,
I beg you that the thing you do, reject.
The land and men of shores America
Are never given to bitter defeat.
So therefore, be you wise and strong and true
And make them country and not colony.

Nay, nay, to give might make desirable to all
The thing one comes to have.
And so would end the state
That is the motherland today.

But they are men, if treated such they would
Be true as any eastern star
And love the mother as a goodly child.

Men! Men! Did they not know
That when they sought those wretched waters for their home
They forfeited all their status being men?
Thus now they are but colony
And have no status but that of a pig
Both born and dead at the word of their lord.

Ah, lord, it is not good for you to talk as such
Nor is it just to call a man a pig,
Nor right to make a man a slave.
My lord, such men are not yours.

Not mine? Mine!
Mine, to throw to the dogs
If I so desired,
Is my soul. Mine to treat
As a slave, if it is my wish.
Do not talk to me of justice,
Of goodness, of right.
There is no justice in a woodland fire
Nor goodness in living
Nor right in death
Mine to throw to the dogs…
And when a man owns another man's soul
Then he is a king.
I am a king.

Have you no mercy?

Speak you not to me of mercy.
Mercy, forgiveness, and truth
Are but for fools.
I am no fool.
They are so valiant now!
But they are poor
And rightly valiant.

Had they but power, then
Their merit full opinion would be worse
And they, like I, would have such anguished dreams
All hell would flee.
Mark well my words, oh, man,
The highest being of the human race
Is idiot indeed to be allowed
The lordship of his fellow man
And cast it hence.
Still, ah, ah, the price is high!
When man rules other men and acts as man
He forfeits to the wind his very soul
(for God and Devil Men will touch it not).
I tell you that I weep at night
"The price is high!"

Then if, my lord, you weep
And as you say is true,
Would man not be more man
And closer to his God,
This cast aside?

Never, never, no!
The lonesome ages past and yet to come
Prove true the thing I prove upon my throne.
E'en had a man a choice,
Which he has not,
The basest coward ever was, would be
The man who knew the price and paid it not.
Full well I know the thing I do
May have for its return a price too high
And make my throne as stable as a man
Who could not ride and yet did mount and whack
An untamed thing.
Still, I would do what I would do
And sent my wholesome armies to the front

To meet some foolish men who in their heads
Have harbored vainer thoughts of right
And freedom and justice.
Oh, if I win, I win. And should I lose,
I lose. Am I to care?

My Guide

Thank God she went before me
Or else I had not gone.
If she had not already walked
If she had not already lived
And lived to guide me through my life
I could not go alone.

Thank God she went before me
And so she knew the way.
And I depended on her strength
And I depended on her love
And I depended on her love
To get me through each day.

Thank God she went before me.
She closed her eyes and fled.
And I am left to mourn my loss
And I fall wounded, scarred, and maimed
And yet rejoice that I am here
And it is she who's dead.

Thank God she went before me
My suffering is the cost.
She loved me deeper than her soul.
She'd not have borne to let me go
The pain of that would wound her so.
Better I stay and she should go,
Better I suffer losing her,
Than that was she who lost.

Epitaph III

I am not here
And not gone to return.
Are any dear,
Or any worth to learn?
I am not here.
But you will have your turn.

Epitaph IV

Let's play at war.
I'll be the south, you the north.
You can kill me, but I won't give up.
I will haunt you, and you'll run
And hide behind your mother.
But your mother is my mother,
And she will spank us both.

Mood

The wind comes quickly through the curtain walls
And grabs my soul. Off o'er the purple leas
The blackened shade so stealthy falls,
Deep violet sky against dark forms once trees.

My soul is gone, my spirit roam
Across enchanted times and space.
Quit sick blue walls that I call home.
Someday I'll meet it face-to-face.

The night creeps in above the haunting cry
Of the black owl whose nest is in my hair.
I now am dead. How sweet to die
And have no coward spirit for its lair.

My soul is gone, my spirit roam
Across enchanted times and space.
Quit sick blue walls that I call home.
Someday I'll meet it face-to-face.

*Love is measured by the length of the pain, Lust by the intensity.

VENGEANCE

The dead do not use vengeance.
They do not try to hurt.
They know the stark finality
Of making someone dirt.

MUSIC

The only music man dislikes
Is that which he himself has made.
Sonatas can be beautiful,
If one refrains from plucking strings.

Remind yourself, when someone says
He would not call such notes a song,
Perhaps he sees his hand around
The pen that wrote the measures out.

My Path

My path is straight, a road so wide,
The yellow line I draw
To walk on in the middle way
Becomes my only law.

And if I sin until I can
Not touch that yellow line,
I do not wrong my God or Man.
It and the sin are mine.

VIEW TO MYSELF

I am not ready to allow this thing
That breathes inside of me access to that
Most royal emotion which my soul
Finds life in and perhaps a bit of death.

I would not rend my heart wide with a pen
For that I now have no controlling of
May one day spite me. Yet my rhymes must be
Most intimate with that which stirs my soul.

So I am forced in small subtleties
To set my guarded thought in timeless ink.
Decreed to show their truth to me alone
And be unfathomed muses to the rest.

My critics frown, I know, on such poor art
But I must lose my name to save my heart.

SNOWFALL

Softly it comes.
Not to be harsh.
Over the valley,
White on the marsh.

Freedom is being
Able to fall
Light on the mountain,
Long in the hall.

Deep Hill

The road to Deep Hill is quite lengthy and wide
With hardly a curve on its course.
The toll for Deep Hill is a piece of your pride.
It often is traveled by force.

The men of Deep Hill boast the road is too free
For any but such as Deep Hill.
But I've been to Deep Hill. It is far beyond me
Why it would give any a thrill.

The road from Deep Hill takes not even a "please"
And happy the ones who stride there,
For the road to Deep Hill must be crawled on your knees.
The ending is only despair.

*One thing you can be sure of—you can never be better than the people you think you are better than.

THE FIRST DAY OF SPRING

Spring now flies on air wings
And with her coming, sadness brings.

It is rumored in Usser
How the youth long to be free
And I smile and wish good fortune
To those brave ones 'cross the sea.
How I mourn because my country
Has no longings such as these.

The sun, it shines
Upon the pines
And diamonds grace their *emeraldry*.
The brown we knew
Like wind birds flew,
Replaced by fair spring's finery.

Oh, to see a green leaf again
Instead of snow that hurts your eyes!
The grass is out after the rain!
I think perhaps the groundhog lies!

The trees that bent so yesterday
Now stand up great and tall.
Oh, how I wish that I could stand
In such a cruel fall!

After the calm, the rain;
After the balm, the pain.

WHAT IS DEATH?

What is death,
   That unknown which all must know?

I do not understand it, nor can tell you;
   But this I know.
   That when I go, I would have something
      Strong and good,
      To lean on,
      When I take that road,
      Be it true or false.

Some people have themselves.
   They go with head held high,
      Ready, waiting,
      Big enough,
      To act whatever comes
      Becoming it.

   But I, I would have something
      Strong and good,
      To lean on,
      When I take that road,
      Be it true or false.

Some people go screaming,
   Crying, fearing,
   Clutching at the rim of life
      Which crumbles in their grasp.
      Crumbles.

But I, I would have something
     Strong and good,
     To lean on,
     When I take that road,
     Be it true or false.

How Do I Leave You

I've labored all this time with you,
How shall I leave you, lifelong friend?
How could I see that blessed rest
And know your toil has yet to end?

Fret not for me. I love you so
I would not see you bent and worn
When blessed peace awaits you where
Our God has called the loved ones home.

Go home, then, love. The Master calls.
Put down your load to rest in peace.
I'll toil on here a little more,
And then I'll join you by and by.

Here at Your Feet

Here at Your feet, I lay my soul,
Poor naked, shivering core of me,
Disrobed of draping of the past,
All I possess, all I could be.

Here at Your feet, I prostrate, pray
For wisdom, Yours, not mine, to do
In that dim time of yet to come
That which Your will assigns me to.

Reptilian, I shed the past
That I more fully godlike grow.
I grieve but never can regret,
This chrysalis that makes it so.

Then onward, layers prized then dropped,
And upward, by Your grace, dear friend,
Until this very world is dropped
And we're united at its end.

Epiphany Eve

Poor wrinkled baby in my arms!
The world gives him his natal bed
With brutal, thoughtless selfishness—
A manger in a rotting shed!

For it is cold and we are poor
And shepherds, being poor as we,
Have given him adoring awe
And shared with us his poverty.

And Joseph, that dear man I love,
Gives him, a bastard, rank of son,
And longs, as I do, for the day
When he is weaned, and we are one.

The birthing blood that gave him life,
The milk that feeds his infancy,
My woman's gifts no man could give,
This woman being womanly.

How easy to be led by God!
Faith pierces rationality!
My God Who made my god-child here
Will keep His tiny family.

Then hush, my heart! Oh, hush, my child!
The love that kept you ever keeps.
Your star still shines! And God provides
Tomorrow's needs while midnight sleeps.

SET GOD SINGING

I want to set God singing
With what I do today.
This is the finest blessing
For which my soul can pray.
I have no better reason
To live or think or be
Than that my God's kind spirit
Rejoices over me.

Oh, let God hear me singing
Above my hurt and fears,
Above my hate and anger
And all my selfish tears.
It doesn't really matter
What sorrow life may bring
As long as how I'm living
Can cause my God to sing.

I want to hear God singing
While my poor spirit lives.
And when I shame God's goodness,
I pray that God forgives.
This is my first ambition
In all I do and say,
To try to set God singing
Today and every day.

Alma Mater

Alma Mater won't appear
Till after she's no longer known.
But then her specter rears its head
And claims the very thoughts we own.

PLAIN OF FEELING

Here on the plain of Feeling
Where emotion's rivers run,
It's here that good fights evil
And the battle is lost or won

Long before the concept
Becomes an established fact
Or ever the raw idea
Has grown into finished act.

Then arm your soul, oh seeker,
Pale pilgrim as it goes
Here on the plain of Feeling
Where emotion's river flows.

TRAVEL

I did not want to go.
My God had said, "You are my child,
Come be with me."
And then God secretly took my hand
And led my eyes into God's eyes
And I saw what God saw.
Oh it was pretty, pretty, fair
And sweet as sky.
But me, I was not satisfied.
I wanted to see what the world saw.
I wanted to be with the world.
It did not matter that the world saw gloom,
And gloom's not as pretty as heaven.
The world is closer to me than God.
I never hear God cry.

Oh, God weeps well enough
And I weep when God weeps
For our souls exist the same.
But the people are calling
And I'm only glad
That I know them both.
What utter hell
To exist entirely on either one of their backs.

ADVENT

It will come to me, like a long-forgotten dream.
Someday, perhaps I shall be old, perhaps young,
Perhaps with experience, perhaps without,
Perhaps wise, perhaps foolish.
I only know that it will come to me,
That I will see it, that I will know it for what it is,
That I will run to it and caress it.
Is it death alone? No,
For it has spoken, has told me it will come.
And death never speaks.

Hymn to God

Deity of my being, commander of stars, believer of souls,
God of sun and rain, God of me;
Teacher, jailer, giver, taker, aid, and hindrance,
Wise and beautiful, holy, and omnipotent,
O Holy Omnipotence, allow me to sing!

Not that You can teach, but that I learn.
Not that You are dead, but that I live.
Not that You made me, but that you are my life.
Not that I am created, but that I am not perfected.
Not that I may die, but that I want for death.
Not that You are vague, but that I have not eyes.
Not that You control all, but that You control more than I.
Not that I cannot see heaven, but that heaven cannot be touched.
Not that You are good, but that I am evil.
Not that You are wise, but that I am foolish
And simple and lack my own moment.
For this, O Holy Omnipotence, allow me to sing!

O Greatest King of my soul
I do lift up my poor voice.
I do praise You, Lord of the Cosmos
And blue sky and white clouds,
Yellow leaves and old cemeteries.
I do honor You with my soul
And call You great and good,
Teacher, jailer, giver, taker, aid, and hindrance,
Wise and beautiful, holy, and omnipotent,
O Holy Omnipotence, thus do I sing!

LIES

Jesus was a liar
For love begets but tears.
It never gives abundant life
But multiplies our cares.

But then he was a rich man.
His dad owned earth and sky.
If love became too hard for him
His God would let him die.

What Have They Done

What have they done
To the days I once knew,
When time was an ivory god?

What have they done
To the Nile in the spring
And rejoicing when Set was abroad?

What have they done
To the steps rimmed in gold
In a temple, the House of the Sun?

And have they denied
Of a pharaoh his dreams
Because all his ruling is done?

They took all the beauty
Of days fast asleep
And woke it to sunlight and day.

And I marvel that things
Proud for thousands of years
Could suddenly bow to decay.

What have they done
To a little gold ring
That a princess once held in her hand?

They have set it apart
From humanity's touch
And the tiny thing's not half so grand.

BRAGGING, GOD?

Bragging, God? Omnipotence
Is such a rare estate
That one can never comprehend
Who trusts himself to fate.

The blind must understand the light
Before he wants to see.
An unknown metal has no price
However rare it be.

CRYING

Oh, up on the hilltop, a baby is crying,
Poor heartbroken child of a mother now lost.
Sleepless and lonely, it pours out its anguish
To all who will listen and heeds not the cost.

The mother has little of time for the young one.
Her heart and her worry are husband and home.
Her man is a drunkard, a drunkard with money,
And he and his money are longing to roan.

She pleads with him, cries to him, fights him, through hopelessness.
Her anger and crying I sense but can't see
As here on the river, I hear but the baby.
It's wailing its story of dark misery.

Oh, mother, my river, you hear not my weeping?
Are you and the people, my father, at strife?
My father's a drunkard with money. I know it.
But have you no thought for my sorrow, my life?

My mother, my river, wide water that bore me
When I was a poet and laughed and was free,
Is it in the nighttime when I stand here weeping
You flow by, in silence and think not of me?

Too Big

My thanks to God for beauty,
The glimpse I had of heaven,
The red orange clouds of evening
Above the green-black tree.

My thanks for revelation
Of what entails my being,
The stature of my wisdom,
The context of my soul.

Were I to climb a mountain,
The one where trees are greenest,
I'd still be small for heaven
And too big to forget.

PRAYER

Dear God,
    Walk close.
    I am undone if you are far.
    Be near.
    Ever near, every day.
    It is only for my well-being is so attained.
And, God,
    Lead me
    From the music and the drunken laughter
    Of life.
    Take me outside
    To the cold night air and let me see the stars.
    Hold my hand.
    And when I return to the party,
O God,
    Let us walk through the door together.

THE HERMIT

I, Je'anne, of the night wind's breath,
Being of age and ready to die;
Having seen Knonilee met with courage by him who is small
And him who is greater scream;
I, Je'anne, having seen the great pestilence
And having lived, have come
To the house of my fathers to die.

I have had wealth, and he who comes after
Will make it his quest. I say no more.
I have had joy and have seen the trees aflame.
I know how the rusty pines bear their white burden
In the months of want.
I have watched the brook, sing lazy songs of gladness.
Just to live was to be happy in the months of great green.
I have understood the bursting hearts of the months of God.
The world brought forth a thousand wondrous colors, all new.
Thus, also, have I seen the great pestilence descend.
A cloud came down which blocked the sun from our sight.
I believe the months took all the glorious things with them
Slowly.
Still, I could not go; I knew it when it started.
So I have come to the house of my fathers to die.

And now I write the elegy the bats will sing.
For I am Je'anne of the night wind's breath,
And have come to the house of my fathers to die.

ADVICE

Love not,
And so you will not hate.
Laugh not,
And so you will not weep.
Hope not,
And so you'll not need fate.
Wake not,
And you will not need sleep.
Live not,
And so how can you die?
See not,
And blindness cannot try.

Bury your soul in the ground
And shun these things:
Love, Hate,
Laughter, Weeping,
Fate, Hope,
Waking, Sleeping,
Life, Death.

But the greatest of these is love.

Conscience

Conscience, like a red-winged tide
Fed by a hundred rivulets
Rolling and playing about his feet,
Has called to him accusingly,
"You did what you did.
What you did, you have done
And your eyes shall not rest
On the cool rising sun."

Conscience lapped about his knees,
Drove him backward with its force,
Called to him, in agony,
Lest it should be left unheard,
"You did what you did.
What you did, you have done.
And you know such low deeds
Are not shown to the sun."

Conscience bathed his body. No
Egyptian mortuary's as sweet.
And he did not naught but shed two tears,
One from each eye, and then he coughed,
"You did what you did.
What you did, 'twas your goal,
Though admittance is hard."
Then the words drowned his soul.

REGRET

I'm sorry that I stayed away.
I knew I should have come
When I stood there atop that hill
And watched the setting sun.

I'd best been with you when you wept
Around my mother's grave.
I should have heard your mourning words
And took the gifts you gave.

But oh, my mother is not there.
She's not beneath that stone.
And do not shed your tears for me
For I am not alone.

My mother's up atop that hill
Watching the setting sun.
I too must go and watch a while
When my poor life is done.

Unafraid

It is fine to be sad.
For the dark, when it comes,
Won't dry your tears.
But to fear, it is almost subhuman.
For you shouldn't wait
Just to cry.

Business

The light was white,
And too pure to be sunshine.
It reflected softly
Off yellow topped tables and chairs,
Always white.
Over beside the door
A furnace hummed and blew,
But no air circulated in the room.
Sunshine isn't felt in business rooms.
They lock the sun outside
And cover the windows
(What for?)
With green and blue curtains.
The light is white fluorescence,
Dustless,
Odorless,
And cold.
No dirt.
No life.
No flowers.

Why is it odd then, cousin?
These dustless, odorless, cold people
Should not be expected to feel.

INSECT

I slew a bug upon my arm.
It didn't do me any harm,
I slew it. I bashed in its head,
For it was red. But now it's dead.
It left a little reddish spot
Upon the place where it is not.
I wish that when I dead shall be
I'd leave a place the size of me.

POET

I cannot paint a picture with my hands.
I can't form subtle greens or brazen blue
With tempera paint. The artist who commands
Such gifts is truly great. That I can't do.

But I can shut my soul up in a box
And let it rest and throb inside awhile
Then take it out and lose its many locks,
And it will sing and make a dead man smile.

PRIME

I thank you, God, for guidance shown
My crude attempting to decide
The issues of my circumstance
But fail the very goals I pride.

I thank you, God, that you are wise
Enough to force my heart to wait.
So often I would forge ahead
Too fast, when I should hesitate.

I thank you, God, for loving me.
Your love shines clearest bathed in time.
Events that manifest your care
Must reach their predetermined prime.

To David

The gift you gave to me, my friend,
When you accept me as I am
And as I am, you nourish me
And beckon me to better things.

Accepting that you give to me,
That unencumbered openness
To what I feel and whom I know,
I value more my knowing you.

The gift you give to me, my friend,
Like any true and perfect gift,
Perfects far more the one who gives
And leaves unworthy who receives.

A Bit and a Piece

I'm a bit and a piece of a meadow in twilight,
A bit and piece and a part.
I'm the rhyme to the song of the lark in the evening,
A rhyme and a flake of its heart.

I'm a silver of moon when it shines on the river,
And a droplet that's part of the stream.
I'm the twinkling smile of a baby that's dreaming
And even a phase of that dream.

I'm the song of a maiden alone with her lover,
And the tune of a mother and child.
I'm the whisper of thunder when death stalks a household,
And the glory of all that is wild.

I am poet and priestess, the seer, the mother,
Too much in the world, too apart.
I'm a bit and a piece and a part of existence
The voice and the mood and the art.

EVOLUTION

They saw God in the evening sky
And in the morning dew.
They saw him in a mountain high
And in a river too.

They sought him as a desert cat
And in the birds on wing.
They cringed that he the sound begat
Of thunder clouds in spring.

They felt a longing in their hearts
And fear of the unknown,
And so with all their simple arts
They carved him in their stone

And asked him for no rain at sea
And sun in haying time,
Destruction for their enemy,
And happiness sublime.

And when his answer didn't come
They slew a calf or child
And offered up that awful blot,
Believing that he smiled.

At last, they saw with wiser eyes
That death brought no relief.
They called him Vengeance. Hating lies,
They called him true belief.

And so they sought him in their wars
And found him partially.
They could have found God anywhere.
God's anywhere, you see.

But gods of war can never help
When you are old and die
Surrounded by your home. They sought
A god of heart to try.

And so they named him Love and taught
And end to death and strife.
The told of love they said had brought
True joy to human life.

They built him temples strong, with locks.
They could not see his whole
Was all. They put him in a box
Restricted unto soul.

CRUCIFY

Oh, mystery that marries to the cross each act I own!
My good would never cause his pain; my evil crucified.
I magnify his torment with the unknown wrongs I do
And when in malice, God, I sin, I pierce his crimson side.
Beside that wedded horror, I, Niobe, prostrate fall.
My very thoughts have killed my friend, in spite of how I cried.

ALGEBRA

I wrote a number on a plain white page.
And then I wrote another and one more.
And these three numbers rose and fought a war
Against an enemy called "line."
Against the line, they fought and won
And crossed the line and habited the place
That once was line, leaving their own sweet place
As barren as a grave. They left the very thing
They fought for.
They became "line."

Before

Before we eat, we must be fed.
Before we live, we must be dead.

SHARON'S

The empty pit I feel inside,
The one that has no floor,
Identifies itself with night
And with the blue gray sky.

I think I'll take my pen in hand
And blacken the abyss.
I'll take the twinkle in my eyes
And fill the sky with stars.

NOTES

Age makes us regret time.

Soul, do not weep at weeping.
Tears water your growing.
Sunshine alone kills this plant.

To the uninitiated,
Poetry is a maze,
Horror in her presence,
Death in her gaze.

It's him who knows her secret,
Who her bosom bares,
That the horror manifests,
That the death prepares.

To R. P. Wolff

I may call you very bad
Because your thoughts aren't mine.
Yes, I may even prove you wrong
That I appear more fine.

All men may call me wise, and yet
Let them say what they can,
When I in malice criticize
Then I am less a man.

Mercy

There are times when the mercy of God is a sword
And you bleed as its sets your heart free.
For the touch of the Master can sometimes bring fire
As He molds us to what we should be.

We must never forget that our Lord's only goal
Is to gather His own to His side.
And our blistering agony's born of ourselves
For we don't want what He will provide.

If we follow, He leads. But He loves us far more.
When we choose our own way, He explains
If we only seek shelter with Him in the storm,
We will dwell in perpetual rains.

*If we did not learn, there would be no death. Learning brings change, and change necessitates death.

CRUCIFIED

O God, I do not love despair,
But would it not be better
To take it rather than a dream,
A bond above a fetter?

I do not ask that punishment
Be me alone denied.
But stop! For I can see no end,
And I am crucified.

BEDTIME

Let us be children of darkness,
For darkness covers all.
Let us sing songs of dusk
For we are tired of death.
Let us forget everything
Except ourselves.
Let us be ghosts,
For we and ours have had a good allotted time,
And it is good to be a ghost.

JUDGMENT

When it's just God and you
Then genetics won't do.
You can't blame Mom and Dad
Or the rough life you've had.
Then accept as a fact
You must own every act
And, for better or worse,
Share the blessing or curse.

MELTED BUTTER

Melted butter used to grow
In that grand primeval vale
Where today flows Ohio
With white water for a sail,
Writhing water for a sail.

Melted butter went away
Too the reddened and the gold
That upon the hillside stay
With the pine trees which were old
When the water was not old.

Man is a leaf on a yellow tree
Falling down through eternity.

JOANIE

Joanie marched through Christendom
With her ten thousand men,
And each man left a pretty bride
To wade around in sin.

They did not care, she did not care.
She led them all away.
Some say that she bewitched them all.
And Joanie's dead today.

WHO

Who will buy the hopes I treasured?
Who will pay for broken dreams?
For I've want of them no longer
And they're death to life, it seems.

"In my house, I've burial for them,"
Said the devil to the sky
And my eyes were wide with wonder.
God said softly, "So have I."

Soul

Each man has his little hell.
Most people call it "soul."
But hell's not always bad. There are times
When heaven and hell are one.
Like when you think you're free
And cry.
They say that Jesus cried.
I don't know
And I'm not wise enough
To hear the thunder when Buddha's teardrops fall,
If they fall.

I don't think "souls" a bad word.
I only curse it because it's there.
There are times when I'm sure I am glad for "soul."
And it's then that people think I'm mad.
When people think I'm mad, it's then
I curse at "soul."
But it can't help it, wretched creature.
It hasn't the power of suicide.

(It's for that reason I pity your heaven.
There is not a man on earth
Who doesn't know sorrow and pain.
But oh, how terrible
To be thrown into joy which you cannot escape.)

An Incident

Pain confronts us often while we live.
The undenying ache we suffer from
When we are faced with that not understood,
Unrealized, and therefore, we're undone.

Fighting makes it worse, forgetting does
But little in its time and when the hurt
Returns, it brings a torment far the worst
Of all those agonies, and we are cursed.

Time and time alone, an age or two,
Can dull the mute bewilderment we feel.
We no more think or reason in such state
Than laugh aloud at silent funerals.

SATAN

I know you, Satan, crueler than the dawn
That shows us what we are and drowns our dreams.
I know you, spiteful, vengeful, lacking love
Or even baser kindness for your peers.
I see you there where crying long prevails.
I see you where the sadist's triumph reigns,
Where fortune grins on what is vilest done,
Where children cry in hunger while asleep
And saints go feasting half a block away.

I watch you cheat your brother for his gold.
I see you create death to punish death.
I watch you in the name of righteousness
Condemn men for the sins that you commit.
Why, Satan, praise a war that kills your sons?
Why make war causeless, the perpetuate
Its ugly blot? But, Satan, you are base.
I know your name.
I know you well; your other name is Man,
And human nature is your other soul.

Something to Think About

I would turn to you when life grows hard
Except that this gross path on which I walk
Is never wide, permitting change in course.
The change must come within my private soul.
And now I'd rather lie secure in brick
That writhe in torment at the heart of night.
Come teach me courage, but I cry, "Beware!"
The trainer who incites a lion's wrath
Is often he who lies beneath its paw.

FAITH

There is no joy incapable of name,
No sweet emotion lacking syllable.
Our tongue is not a foreign thing to love,
Nor hate nor all the myriad in between.

Yet there are no doubt complexities of sound,
Which do defy uneducated tongues
Or those with knowledge, not experience,
Being too new to life to comprehend
The subtler reasoning of minute variety.

Say not, though thoughts lie unexpressed as words,
The words are nonexistent. Such is false.
Stupidity's a poor excuse for lack
Of than which people say makes children men.

MY WAY

I did not take the lonely road
Because I feared a road more wide,
Or scorned the people whose abode
Is rimmed in roses on each side.

I took that road because that way
Is that to which I have been born.
I'd no more in the flowers stay
Than wish my soul a crown of thorns.

And though I be both crowned and thorned
I cannot choose but here remain
Along this lonely road, a scorned
And destined soul of human bane.

Oh, woe! But you, you took this road
Because of scorn. I say not nay
For heavier had been my load
Had you not passed along my way.

GRAY BLUE

Gray blue water
Shaded by hills
Shyly opening
Yellow green.

Wind in the trees,
Barren and brown,
Plucks at the yellow green
Promise of spring.

LETTER

I think that I shall go apart and die.
If epitaphs be eyes for eyeless skulls,
Then reader watch. This is my epitaph
And I see you as clearly as you see
This printed page. The people of this world
Are greater, dearer, sweeter fools than I.
Beware! I say not to myself alone
"I am not mad." It testifies it's false.

I think that I shall go apart and die.
Goodbye, oh, world, called cruel and sweet and great.
You have not known me, world, so much is best.
I have not known of you as I should know.
To speak in single terms would cause much pain.
(And who am I to speak of pain and hurt?)
Oh, world, I only say I am too deep for you
And you too wide for me. Dare I say more?

When such conditions rise, they warrant act
And parting is the only act dare come.
No doubt had I not parted on my own
My own would have me parted from itself.
Be proud, I died and called you all my own!

To Two

One does not wait for happiness.
He goes and finds it out.
He dusts his heart and sits prepared
Without a single doubt.

It puzzles me, magnanimously,
That if it houses there
It always brings along its twin,
Joy's only harm, despair.

Saturday and Debussy

The hell that I walked through,
Because I did not know that I was free
To walk or stay,
The hell that I walked through!
I would not retrace my path for all the childhoods that this
world has known.
Whatever follows,
Be it bad or worse,
Whatever comes
To me and all the things I know,
I'll face calmly
With my eyes wide open.
And I'll walk whatever road was made for me
Because I have the freedom to walk or stay.

Worship cannot exist without growth. If your concept of God
remains stagnant for five years or five months, then it is not worship
anymore.

God grants us that place beyond death where we are all made
perfect, and love is the rule, not the exception.

About the Author

Dr. Rosanna Lowther-Berman (George Washington University, 2004) worked as a Teacher and Special Education Director in both Ohio and West Virginia. She has also worked for the West Virginia Department of Health and Human Resources (WVDHHR) in various capacities. She was the liaison for the closing of some state hospitals and the deinstitutionalization of individuals housed therein. She has also worked as a surveyor for West Virginia ICFs/IID, Behavioral Health Centers, Opioid Clinics, and, prior to 2006, Residential Childcare Facilities. She worked for West Virginia Advocates following her retirement from WVDHHR until returning part-time to the WVDHHR Bureau for Medical Services as Program Manager for the Waiver State Transition Plan. She also does consulting work, primarily on Policy and Complaint Investigations. Dr. Lowther-Berman resides in Charleston, West Virginia, with her two dogs and one cat.

www.ingramcontent.com/pod-product-compliance
Lightning Source LLC
Chambersburg PA
CBHW071017120626
46546CB00003B/1124